IMPURE THOUGHTS
Golnoosh Nour

VERVE
POETRY PRESS
BIRMINGHAM

PUBLISHED BY VERVE POETRY PRESS
https://vervepoetrypress.com
mail@vervepoetrypress.com

All rights reserved
© 2022 Golnoosh Nour

The right of Golnoosh Nour to be identified as author of this work has been asserted in accordance with section 77 of the Copyright, Designs and Patents Act 1988.

No part of this work may be reproduced, stored or transmitted in any form or by any means, graphic, electronic, recorded or mechanical, without the prior written permission of the publisher.

FIRST PUBLISHED NOV 2022

Printed and bound in the UK
by Imprint Digital, Exeter

ISBN: 978-1-913917-21-0

Cover illustration by Sailor Stephens
insta: sailors.ghost

CONTENTS

Astrological Storms	8
Inventing Language	9
Cheap Tricks	11
Scorpio Sun	12
The Cursed Art of Storytelling	13
Religion	16
Anxious Dreams of Ambitious Little Deaths	17
Dogs Masquerading as Wolves	18
Cemetery	19
Dirty Moon	20
Men with Small Mouths	21
Reliquary	22
Vexed Vixen Tale	23
Let the Darkness Speak	24
Ode to Courage	25
Of Rumours and Regrets	27
Today Is the Day	28
Curious Circumstances	29
Juxtaposition	30
Towards Gods	31
Your Blood	32

Acknowledgements

'Desire is no light thing.'
–Anne Carson

'Toys, pets, boys... Inside each enchanting exterior was a vagueness that disappointed me night after night.'
–Dennis Cooper

'I had a presentiment then that there is in this world a kind of desire like stinging pain.'
–Yukio Mishima

IMPURE THOUGHTS

Astrological Storms

I am what they call ex tremely bi sexual
'extremely' for I can only be an extremity or a non-entity
'What is a man? What is a woman?' Asked Mishima
in 1950. 'What are genders and sexualities?' I ask in 2020.
And before I know it, I realise I am a woman stuck in a sacred circle,
asked to pray, to work, to learn. And before I know it, I dream I
am a boy desperate for the dark men of my dreams. There is a list, but
only a few can make it. My lovers agree on one thing – that I stink.
I bathe in mirrors, moonbeams, and blossoms, so perhaps I only stink of
Treachery for I cannot be loyal to ideas, to diets, to deities, even
to my astrological signs; I justify my mood swings
and storms of heart by my Gemini moon like a basic bitch from Starbucks
but my Taurus sun makes me carry my assurance like a torch.
My brother says, how are you so sure?
How can you be so certain whom and what you want?
His Virgo sun analyses everything until we both bleed.
He is eternally ambivalent, pensive, and pained
I am profoundly impulsive, explosive, and pained
two wrecked emotion machines, we are twins.
We stroll around every nasty city we are allowed
in, holding hands, pretending we own every land
we step on like a pair of otherised yet middle-class snobs.
I know I have been fetishised but I'm a fetishist myself.
He loves his sad modernists, and I revel in my egregious
transgressionists. We explore each other as we enter the light.
I realise it is my lack of ambivalence that makes me stink.
This assurance of mine means when I desire something,
the urge is strong, and when I'm supposed to desire something
but the urge is non-existent, I cannot even feign interest.

Despite acting all young and fluid, I'm stuck in my old ways
like a blind bull in stormy weathers.

Inventing Language

I have no desire to process this
I have every desire to pretend it doesn't exist
but I smile, flashing my blunt teeth, unable to connect the dots.
These dots are our enemies; they murdered my mother, and now

they are after us. These dots are not even dots
they're needles, swords piercing my veins and your brain.
Your toothless smile is insanely visceral – you used to look like me.
Your brain, once an Adorable Dad brain, a professor

brain, a mathematical brain, a love brain is darkening and I
refuse to understand the science behind this blasphemy.
Your madness isn't the kind that attracts me; it is destroying me.
Despite this you still call me beautiful and tell me you love me

then boast to your nurse that I have invented a new language,
while this is embarrassing, I let this be my meaning of poetry.
But you don't stop – you never knew how to stop –
you moan that you're bored that you want to take me out for

'a walk, find that special tree, and pick the best pomegranate' for me. I
listen to your discursive stories in the mad hope of recreating our sacred
narratives, but it selfishly occurs to me that you have failed me.
You get angry at me – as if you read my thoughts – tell me I am a liar

and I should live with you 'right now!' You wail as you recall the death
of my mother – her powdered corpse, eternally fresh in your mind –
I am transfixed at the horrors of our lives.
Your nurse is consoling you; I find he is becoming more and

more beautiful as I am getting roaringly ugly.
He is now your favourite child, and I
just another failed daughter, surreptitiously irate and as
deranged as her beloved father

Cheap Tricks

I always wanted it darker – harder
the bushes and the pines weren't enough
sexuality is and isn't about genitalia, head
bursts with its hysterics every night
and bisexuality, my sinister saviour, whispers
a hard cock could be a hard clit, and vice versa.

Sometimes one eats when one is famished, other times
to possess a sensation, to repress another urgency. You
bit into your carrot cake, catching my hungry eyes, then licked
the cream off your pink lips, your tactics cheap
like the cake you were devouring, but that didn't stop me
for cheapness has seldom stopped me – I am a hard
snob only on the outside, my insides
are as soft as baby teeth; I am indeed
weak and my desire is as thin as your fingers so
when you put them inside me, I trembled.

We both felt like cheap cheats, but I'd say it was worth it
 —   my orgasm was delicious just like your cheap cake.

Scorpio Sun

I made   love   to myself thinking   of you   your voice inside my phone   this crisp seduction   wrongly tuned   disastrous errors taste better my mind is made of mdma   it tells me impurity is the only pure state   this time my desire is simple: I want   to open my door   for you   wide and shameless   I want   to sit extremely   close to you   in a lacklustre dinner party   without anyone noticing   without being close to you   I want   to touch your lips without knowing your words   I don't want to listen to you   I want your   words   inside me   as they become a   scorpion   your hard poison is my obsession   I want   it   inside me   without being polluted   I dream   about having you and cleaning myself after   I dream   about wiping off your   marbled cum from my chest like pure dirt   I dream   about our whispering silences   the beauty and secrecy   of pure dirt   I   don't want it nice and sweet for if I want sweetness   I eat a fucking candy   two candies   ten even   I want to die in my extremities   I want   to choke   on unnecessary escalation   on my sickly excitements   my impure thoughts and desires   and their ruin ous consequences

What would Jesus say?
What would Allah say?
Most importantly, what would Mother say?

Oh   but I am bored   of being stuck on this whizzing escalator   your presence: sudden and perverse   has purified the air   I want you   dark hard ethereal   a poisoned present   just   promise to leave me after   I want   to be feverish and ravenous   for the rest of forever   and   when I demand, 'when will you fuck me,'   I want you   to whisper

'Tomorrow, 6:36 pm, when I'm alone, and you're unclean.'

The Cursed Art of Storytelling

These sickly days, I desire so hard I give
myself migraines, pains that make me hallucinate

see visions, aches that fill my face like rain, but I
will not stop thinking about sex

during the past few years, I have only desired
three men, which makes me feel chaste

the only thing they have in common is that
they're all unavailable. This unholy trinity comprises

a gay man, a married man, and a bisexual twink.
The gay and the married are both thirty years older than me, but

I prefer them both to my decadent twink.
How this has happened is inexplicable to me.

I have to focus on the dead-end of my 9 to 9 job, but
I'm constantly vibrating, like my phone, a total whore

the married man sees me in public places
to talk about death and our favourite novels and

his wife calls 66 times during our two-hour novelistic talk.
He is apologetic, but I am so wet and thrilled I

don't mind. I rush to the public bathroom and
the evidence is clear – there is a flood.

When I return to our table, he asks
me if he makes me nervous as he strokes

my sweaty hands with his lithe fingers and dark eyes, and I suffice
to say *maybe*. I apologise for my sweat, slip

my hands away, and rant about my dead mother (again) and my strange
desires for the strange gay angel. Elsewhere, I tell my desired gay about

my desire for the confused twink and bore him to death.
At midnight, through the smokes of our wine,

I whisper to the twink that his scandalous story
is making me sick as I playfully

pretend to choke him; I profess his chaos excites and
sickens me as I pull his ponytail that falls apart in my palm.

He says we're just a typical pair of traumatised sluts in
need of morals as he gifts me a repressed kiss. Why do I do this?

This endless desire for unachievable pleasure,
for flirting so badly you make your crush vomit.

I need to throw away my life, reinvent myself through
masquerading my traumas as drama. I want to stop this existence and

Start all over again. A historic chance to change my name
my shame, my games, my pasts, presents, and the futures

Romanticism only works as a literary school, not a way of life.
When I was growing up, I should've read less literature

and other useless arts, instead I should've studied self-help
and survival tactics during capitalism and colonisation for people

with Byronic visions, Persian temperaments, wrong names,
wrong borders, wrong years, wrong sexes.

But I am also happy I don't have a penis, and sometimes I'm happy
I educated myself through Romanticism – not self-help –

there is no dichotomy, and I'm not looking down on anything, but
thank you very much I'd rather be a lost libertine than a 'thriving' liberal.

Still, I am an expert in denial. Wetness is my superior secret,
and I will take it to my grave before confessing my impure sensations.

Religion

Here   there's no more analyses   temporalities   ethics   Only
sens   ations   urges   and accidents   She
is the   Lucifer of my dreams   all flesh and instinct   and I've
been   throbbing since we met the light   was dark   the day was gone
                                                                and   she
stroked my   thighs

It is true that desire can get in the way of life   be impossible   deranged
desire   might even kill   I'm not lucky but I owe it to her to be faithful
                                                                               to myself

and when she's writhing and screaming   under my tongue
when she bruises my breasts
I finally feel   religious   out of this world   freed

                                          transcendent

Anxious Dreams of Ambitious Little Deaths

People like us die young living on

      the border |_|

    in the depths of the iceberg

              of nostalgia euphoria lamentation

orgasmic infants until the end   tears of joy and hunger
self-sabotage our drug, we are   quick to burn, to melt, to fly
we are our own myth [s]

      our own dream
      our own deaths

    we are dreaming/ dying/ flying we

    can't tell the difference

people like us   rush rule run   until   they die.

There is no pause – the sun awaits   us

the ground slipping away

our weight is   ecstatic, heavy, and light

we are made of gold and garbage, of a desire to burn:

    No balance – we only fall asleep during blood,

high-per on the dream of the dream of our little deaths
we crash   into the sky ------------------

Dogs Masquerading as Wolves

I was not cursing, but cruising
looking for a boy
ethereal and deranged
as you, for this danger is easier than confessing,
'I miss you,' or 'I'm sorry I hurt you,' or worst of all
'You hurt me,' yes, it is my portentous pride, my
anaemic violence, the arrogance of my flesh, this glass
shield of mine will eventually cut me – a happy ending –
my head is full of death already.

Cemetery

Always, I end up in ruins, no
matter where I start; I must
be taking the wrong pills, the
wrong boys, the wrong schedules; I
must've said yes to a murderous tendency.

The ruins might be warm or cold, I prefer them
hot, so I can sweat all my urges that are choking me
—   a serpent around my neck – I don't think I
am even breathing correctly. Mother should've killed
me when I was a foetus, not when I was a teen.

Mother! I'm still bleeding, why can't you hear me
scream? Listen to my blood, and it will
confess what we've done wrong.

Dirty Moon

It is the small things: the
I get wet when I look at these sculptures.
The fact that you know all
the signs and symbols: a lily on an ancient
Persian soldier made of stone – with eyes like yours.

But on that day, nothing is as radiant as your eyes:
Two emerald moons consuming me,
and as if this isn't enough, you make me photograph
your marble thighs in glittering daylight.
And then comes the thrilling disruption:

You slurp your squid and gaze at me, stating,
You're so spoilt I want to suck you off.
I too want to lick you, but we're exiles, all wrong times,
tongues, breasts, and traumas. All nostalgia and betrayal.
The heat is as unforgiving as our country, and

your obsession with analyses hurts my instincts,
but your philosophy is both ironic and iconic,
and our dirty talk feels spiritual in our mother tongue.
When we kiss, we are خيس khis, and it's even better than
my mirror dreams: our bodies liquefy, swell, and

heat up as they become an exploding sun, and
it feels like the end of times; your skin emits
a certain wet heat that's melting my insides and out.
The moon is bursting full, and we
gasp hard as the moonlight enters our cunts.

Men with Small Mouths

Soft, salmon pink, ready to devour
mysterious slightly mad maddening

in their ambivalence, the latent enthusiasm
subtle like a lethal weapon

overflowing with words that make
No sense, desire dripping from their tongue

also small, subdued yet ready to explore
eager for more for lies untold

a small mouth, pinkish, selfish, greedy
reminiscent of the damaged boy within
the little boy, full of life and loss – like me.

Reliquary

I am   ugly

I don't have many lovers other than:

raw carrots

celery: raw or stewed

extremely   fleshy olives: their salt   penetrate my tongue

Granny   Smith: its sourness   blunting my teeth

ripe mango: its gold urine   running down my chin

juicy pomegranate: its blood   staining my skin   and this murder
                                                                                makes me sexy

Medjool dates: sweeter than any date   their sweetness   hurts my
                                                                                         throat

garlic: its stench makes me an addict

mushroom: to feel magic

nicotine: I get   high   purr   for I need to be hyper and smell like my
                                                                                                                    father.

Oh, also my country of birth has betrayed me, so has my country of residency. They have both betrayed me on multiple occasions, and they will continue to
                                                                                                                          do so.

I shall always eat and smoke to burn the relics of both.

Vexed Vixen Tale

Trouble is there was a time when
all them boys wanted you & you wanted them all, so you got none.
Or maybe God exists & you were punished for your greed.
Now all those boys emerge into one species, a winged angel
who flies away, slipping through your grip like lukewarm water in winter.

You, naïve vampiric vixen, needed to learn to push & not push, you needed to learn to act pretty, to smile just enough – not too little, not too much – to sharpen your teeth on time, instead of waiting for the fate to get on your side – it never was.
You should've jumped when you ran and run when you jumped.

In short, you did everything wrong.

Let the Darkness Speak

After Isidore Ducasse: Comte de Lautréamont

Listen! I am the son of Filth: I obeyed Mother and inherited an instinctive and extreme cruelty that has made me all the more angelic. I am convinced by evil and you will thrive, you will become a star in the starless sky if you take my advice: Conceal your darkness from the masses, not me. Let me hook my claws into the scabs on your scurvy nape. Let us relish my criminal oil, let my moonbeams make the tomb's marble gleam, I am a radiant angel, my magnificent palace is built of silver walls, golden columns, and diamond doors. Worship my pernicious presence, for I, with my angel's wings, with my sinful intensity, only I know how your sins put us in the most virtuous situation. Sanction the sadness, inject the joy that comes with sucking, sticking anything into anything, absorption of skin, anything sacrilegious anything sick and sardonic is sacred to me, for I am the one who sniff the ashes of past lovers, I who murdered my shame in the sea, I am sand and I am sane, I grow darkness within me. You might cut my tongue, but I have sharp teeth and shark sex, my allure is in – inside you already – and in vincible. I burst into fits of laughter like a hyena, I received life like a wound, so I kiss the sea, weeping, for I defied death and divine vengeance with a supreme howl, I am on the dark side of my selves, of your selves, my slave (s), say my name – a ritualistic prayer in a horror game. Take my advice, and you will be wickeder than I! I am the idol that breaks itself, I am the sin that slaughters himself, I am the soil that stains herself, I am the dark celebration of your virtuous lover's death. I am the glorious collapse of an empire in decay, I am the sin, the scenery, the sacrilege, the only rule, and rupture.

> I shall break you
> and you
> will beg
> for it.

Ode to Courage

For Sasha Dovzhyk

I've never written about courage
or other honourable matters.
Here's the first arrow I shall throw
godlessly praying that my weak poison
will obliterate your tactless enemies
and keep you safe.

You know me – you have read me
with your eyes – jade emerald and gold: forests on fire
I first saw you almost a decade ago within
the suffocating perimeter of a university, which was
always too small for you – even my first impression was
you looked jarringly radiant in that dull space!

A university was good enough for me for I have been
a complacent thief, living on feeble hysterics, my first solution
is always escape; I know loss happens in a second, and
when I drink a perfectly warm cup of black tea or
eat a home-cooked meal or paint my lips like a battlefield,
my animal satisfaction makes me ignoble and ecstatic.

I desire so many things that sometimes I think I need nothing.
But nothing was good enough for us. We were that:
Youth and beauty made us divine and unholy – you and I were
favourite targets of envy, but I didn't realise
how much courage you camouflaged
in your joyous decadence!

I thought you were like me, secretly apathetic, anxiously snobbish,
controlled by fear, an eternal escapee, sheltering with us
cowards in peacock feathers, in apocalyptic hyacinths, in cowardly
lack of politics, in bland western sushi, in nonsensical theories, in
Beardsleyesque dreams, in leathery cocktails, in
this monstrous capitalism, away from the real world on fire.

But you carry the salve, a different kind of fire.
You spread it like sunrays in a generous summer
I now understand we are not alike.
I was born to leave; I left to escape, no love was drunk
enough to keep me in a country that was falling away from me.
It is true – I threw away my country like used condoms.

To protect myself from further wounds, I discard people
at my first moments of inconvenience, and god knows
I count the seconds to dispose of myself.
I've discarded myself too many times
to count, often
in cowardly manners.

I am not as valiant as you, but I know how it feels when
something sublime and precious gets attacked, torn, threatened;
it is maddening. You had to leave – by ferry!
There was no other path vast enough for you.
I am now old enough to know I know nothing
about anything, but old enough to know your departure
from our unimpressive safety into glorious flames is what courage means.

You left to stay, to fight to bring the fire the sun the light
I saw how you abandoned this petty safety of ours,
how you've been risking to love, and in short, I was shocked.
But despite my violent shame, I am proud of the golden pen you
gifted me before you left for your courageous destination:
a country I have learned and loved through you. Now
I whisper your cities like a religious chant: Mariupol, Kharkiv, Lviv.

Of Rumours and Regrets

The rumours are often correct
I was born with regrets. The largest one:
In that sizzling café: when he stretched his neck towards me
over our table so I'd smell his cologne (something *Noir*, in fact I
remember the exact brand, but this is not a perfume advert, it is a
poem, or at least it is begging to be one) when he threw his neck at
me to smell it/ him, I should've kissed it!
The scented throat of his, my lips full of quivering hysterics
a kiss of mine might've slashed his throat but
it would've been worth it.
And this revelatory regret only comes to me
a week a month a year after the lost moment when
I'm in the bath, dirty and sick like
a drugged-up visionary.

Today is the Day

Nobody kisses me, nobody even looks at me
today I am earnest and candid – almost needy
shivering before a screen, smoking it, squalid

I admit that x isn't a kiss, and o isn't a hug, xo
sounds like a game, a game my ex won.

                              No

I won't be touched, missed, or kissed, and this

self-pitying possibility is so sad it's almost soothing.

Today I am unable to breathe, to perfume my skin,

my cologne smells like a colony about to burn

I am emptied, expired, dry already like my land sticky & no rain can

wash me clean.

Curious Circumstances

We speak every sunrise, and every moonrise you leave
our screens and enter my dreams, continuing our conversation:
Some poems never end – and I have other brothers, too

other beautiful, bruised men who know how to speak
but only you and I were there when Mother stated,
'Pomegranate purifies the blood; eat!'

As if our blood had been unclean, and then she herself
died of unclean blood, in curious circumstances.
But our life is a curious circumstance.

You and I suffered from both curiosity and circumstance
when others praised learning, we avoided knowledge, we didn't
want to know that we were unclean, about to be

punished by Parents, God, Relatives, and other authorities.
We had no desire to know that we needed
Purification. We didn't want to know mother was dead

leaving us eternally unclean.
Now, I knife pomegranates, expecting pure blood, but
every perfection seems diseased to me, and I

know this is because my eyes are unclean – just like my blood –
and my rotting body in exile, and your sacrificial self
in our scarlet land, feeding pieces of your flesh to our falling father.

Juxtaposition

You wanted me but I   desired your boyfriend
sex   uality shouldn't be studied   it should just be
when your boyfriend writes to me   I only respond by
touching   me   whether he reads me or not   is not my responsibility
either way   I don't understand sexuality   especially   mine
past lovers   have accused me   of being   an angel-headed demon
a clueless princess   a depressed prince   an ecstatic dictator   a vanilla slut
only because   I want what I want when I want it
and this dawn   your   weak boyfriend   visited me again
this time in my dreams   asking me   to join him   in a distant
battlefield   and I admit I was tempted   just because
it doesn't take much to tempt me
my glitch is I either want no boys or I want them all
What would a girl do with just one boy? Breed like bacteria? Give birth? Die?
Get tangled up and suicidally bored?
With two boys one can do more. Three? Even better.
I don't ever want to perish especially from the disease of ordermarriagestructure
but in my dream   your boyfriend   and I did   not   enter
the battlefield   we were both   trapped   in a feast   a festive conversation
I am tired restless bloodless   I am   losing   the   battle   of my own
body   I can hardly exist   I shall not go to the battlefield   I told him

What does your seductive boyfriend represent?
Why a bloodied battlefield?
And why do I address you instead of him?

Desire is in flux   so perhaps
You could take my hand
drag me out of my conflicted skin
burn my skull into the ground

Make me breathe

Towards Gods

I turn my mouth into a wound
my eyes into the moon
before leaving the nest

one never knows what urges
await our surrender
and what desires our permission

but I am the only one I contradict
by carrying myself from one battle
to the next, I am tired and obscene

trembling through my shameless
powers, painful and impure
in my godless quest for purity

Your Blood

For Mahsa Amini

At school, wrapped in a confused childhood and hijab
I was taught that the blood of the innocents will bite

I was taught many things: poetry, the importance of purity, the Holy
Quran. But now everything is a scarlet fog, a burnt flag, a dead ghazal

a fuck I didn't give. The blood of the innocents stayed with me
for I never believed the myth; everywhere around me

evil was cackling, unfolding, triumphing, and I was a sickly
child, forced to shelter inside my family's middle-class rut

even now, rotting in my thirties, riding high on the vicious
capitalism of exile, I still carry the air of a spoilt cub

and I shall never learn how poetry got imprisoned inside
the schools, when it was born on the streets, drenched in blood

but you the blossoming fawn of Kurdistan! The eyes of Iran
You had to come all the way to my injured birth city

our deranged Tehran, for what? To innocently visit
with your beloved brother by your side. I know how sibling love

can make one feel invincible and warm, yet they pushed
your brother away, grabbed you, trapped you in their "moral"

dungeons. They split your skull, and joked that you were
murdered by a "stroke". We screamed as we saw your

mother throw herself inside your grave. What did Tehran
give you? A pain worse than the diseases it gifted us ¬

it bequeathed you with death as 'death to the dictator!'
was murmured, seeped into the pollution, became an explosion

and now our surreptitious chant has penetrated every surface of
existence. The Wicked Capital killed you, but the immortal song

of the protest is correct: "you aren't dead, your name is a secret" the
only holy symbol needed for our rituals – an enraged victory will shine.

Oh, Angel of our Revolution! Zhina! Mahsa, the eternal moon in
the dark! Unlike us greying crows, you will be an evergreen

your roots even more ferocious than their satanic verses
your blood, innocent and shattered made us feel so alive with

rage we're burning our capital with all its mortal gods!
And I learned one thing after all:

The blood of the innocents can set a wrong(ed) country
on the flames of
                                  Hell

ABOUT THE AUTHOR

Golnoosh Nour is the author of *The Ministry of Guidance and Other Stories* (2020) and *ROCKSONG* (2021), both shortlisted for the Polari Prize. She's performed her work in literature festivals and events across the UK and internationally. Her work has also been published by Granta, Vintage, and Columbia Journal. Golnoosh teaches Creative Writing at the University of Reading.

Twitter: @DrNourrr
Instagram: golnooshnour

ABOUT VERVE POETRY PRESS

Verve Poetry Press is a quite new and already award-winning press that focussed initially on meeting a local need in Birmingham - a need for the vibrant poetry scene here in Brum to find a way to present itself to the poetry world via publication. Co-founded by Stuart Bartholomew and Amerah Saleh, it now publishes poets from all corners of the UK and beyond - poets that speak to the city's varied and energetic qualities and will contribute to its many poetic stories.

Added to this is a colourful pamphlet series, many featuring poets who have performed at our sister festival - and a poetry show series which captures the magic of longer poetry performance pieces by festival alumni such as Polarbear, Matt Abbott and Genevieve Carver.

The press has been voted Most Innovative Publisher at the Saboteur Awards, and has won the Publisher's Award for Poetry Pamphlets at the Michael Marks Awards.

Like the festival, we strive to think about poetry in inclusive ways and embrace the multiplicity of approaches towards this glorious art.

www.vervepoetrypress.com
@VervePoetryPres
mail@vervepoetrypress.com